Anger Management for Parents

Thinking about the adverse consequence of outrage and brutal conduct on the psychological well-being of people, any strained and antagonistic mother-kid connection could genuinely influence kid improvement and family prosperity. As per various examinations, outrage and forcefulness are an encounter that kids gain from their current circumstance. In this way, guardians can be a model of savagery for their kids (Smith, 2004, Paterson, DeBaryshe, and Ramsey, 1989). Specialists recognize that variables like family frailty, poor disciplinary activities, lacking parental help, and guardians' fierce among the main elements causing brutality in youngsters.

Table of Contents

How to Manage Your Emotions & Raise a Happy and Confident Child

What is emotion?

Emotions are biological states associated with all of the nerve systems brought on by neurophysiological changes variously associated with thoughts, feelings, behavioral responses, and a degree of pleasure or displeasure.

Tips to get you through your emotions

1.   Take a look at the impact of your emotions. Intense emotions aren't all bad.

2.   Aim for regulation, not repression.

3.   Identify what you're feeling.

4.   Accept your emotions

5.   Keep a mood journal.

6.   Take a deep breath.

7.   Know when to express yourself.

8.   Give yourself some space.

Firstly, if parents want to give their children a gift, the best thing they can do is to teach them to love challenges, be intrigued by mistakes, enjoy effort, and keep on learning. That way, their children don't have to be slaves of praise. They will have a lifelong way to build and repair their own confidence.

As guardians, we as a whole need to bring up sure youngsters who flourish and become capable. However, for quite a long time, nurturing specialists had it all off-base as they accepted that certainty and self-esteem could be helped by commending kids with words, for example, 'You're brilliant' what's more, 'All around done'. Broad exploration done somewhat recently shows that this can be negative and surprisingly harmful to youngsters. Other exploration shows that self-esteem comes from the 'back to front as opposed to from the words we decide to utilize when speaking with our youngsters.

So if adulating kids with 'Great kid' or 'You're so cunning' doesn't work, does this imply that we can't impact our kids' certainty and confidence at all? Well, fortunately, the most recent nurturing research shows that there are viable approaches to support kids' confidence and certainty and augment their odds of long-haul achievement. So this current book's goal is to outfit you with apparatuses that will assist you with building up your youngsters' certainty and confidence to make them savvier, stronger, and better ready to adapt to life's difficulties.

Confidence and certainty are firmly related, and we need a sound level of both to have the option to adapt to the difficulties of life and the entirety of its unavoidable 'high points and low points. Confidence is our intellectual and, most importantly, passionate evaluation of our value. More than that, it is the lattice through which we think, feel, and act, and this reflects and decides our connection to ourselves and to other people. While confidence is a significant conceptual idea since it is an impression of our internal identity, certainty is identified with activity and how we relate or draw in with the outer world around us. Certainty can be learned and created; we can turn out to be better at something through training also, redundancy. Yet, an undeniable degree of certainty alone probably won't be sufficient for an individual to flourish and especially to be upbeat because an individual can be certain in one aspect of their lives and unconfident in another. Without a doubt, it is workable for an individual to have high fearlessness and low confidence - and an absence of confidence can be especially harmful. Since albeit an individual with a significant degree of certainty is bound to take advantage of lucky breaks and take on new difficulties, regardless of whether the result is fruitful, on the off chance that they need confidence they may not have a positive outlook on - or reward themselves - for their accomplishments.

An undeniable degree of certainty and confidence are both keys to being effective in all parts of life, both individual and expert. They assume a huge part in how we think and feel about ourselves and our conduct will in general mirror those contemplations and sentiments, regardless of whether they end up being positive or negative. We begin to create certainty and confidence during the early stages and this is significantly affected by our folks' communications with us. For a kid to build up a sound level of both, they need to feel that they are adored by the individuals who are nearest to them and have a solid faith in their abilities. This permits kids to approach new difficulties with certainty and better prepare them to have the option to adapt to damage, dissatisfaction, and disappointment.

As one would expect, research shows that youngsters with significant degrees of certainty and confidence will in general be freer and are bound to perform well at school and develop to become upbeat and fruitful grown-ups. They additionally will, in general, be more brilliant, not because they normally have a higher IQ - which is just one proportion of insight - than their friends, but since they have acclimatized that their insight and capacities can be created and improved after some time, as you will find in this book. While confidence levels do, will in general change marginally at various phases of a youngster's turn of events, it's essential to have the option to perceive the signs if your kid is inadequate with regards to trust in his/her capacities. This could be because of a few outer impacts that are outside of your control, or it very well may be because of a negative experience that your youngster has had. Whatever the basic reason might be, youngsters with low confidence ordinarily need trust in their capacities and tend to 'work themselves out of attempting new things. This is because they are frequently so scared of committing errors that they will in general try not to take on new challenges inspired by a paranoid fear of not being 'sufficient'.

Fortunately, there are steps that each parent can take to help create and sustain your kid's certainty and confidence, to help increment their levels of collaboration and expand their odds of developing to turn into free and strong grown-ups. The initial step is just by getting more mindful of the effect your words and activities have upon how your youngster feels about themselves, and that is by and large what this book is intended to help you do. It will tell you the best way to keep away from a few of the most well-known 'nurturing traps', for example, over- commending and propelling through remunerations. This book gives you powerful options that will help you create and support your youngster's certainty and confidence and boost their odds of developing to become cheerful and skilled grown-ups. A significant degree of certainty and confidence are both keys to being effective in all parts of life, both individual and expert. They assume a huge part in how we think and feel about ourselves and our conduct will in general mirror those contemplations and emotions, regardless of whether they end up being positive or negative.

We begin to create certainty and confidence during the earliest stages and this is enormously impacted by our folks' collaborations with us. For a kid to build up a sound level of both, they need to feel that they are cherished by the individuals who are nearest to them and have solid confidence in their capacities. This permits youngsters to approach new difficulties with certainty and better prepare them to have the option to adapt to damage, dissatisfaction, and disappointment. As one would expect, research shows that kids with significant degrees of certainty and confidence will, in general, be freer and are bound to perform well at school and develop to become glad and fruitful grown-ups. They additionally will, in general, be more intelligent, not because they normally have a higher IQ - which is just one proportion of insight - than their companions, but since they have absorbed that their knowledge and capacities can be created and improved over the long run, as you will find in this book.

While confidence levels do will in general vary somewhat at various phases of a kid's turn of events, it's imperative to have the option to perceive the signs if your kid is deficient with regards to trust in his/her capacities. This could be because of a few outer impacts that are outside of your control or it very well maybe because of a negative experience that your kid has had. Whatever the hidden reason might be, kids with low confidence commonly need trust in their capacities and tend to 'work themselves out of attempting new things. This is because they are regularly so terrified of committing errors that they will in general try not to take on new challenges because of a paranoid fear of not being 'sufficient'.

Fortunately, there are steps that each parent can take to help create and sustain your youngster's certainty and confidence, to help increment their levels of collaboration and expand their odds of developing to turn into autonomous and tough grown-ups. The initial step is basically by getting more mindful of the effect your words and activities have upon how your youngster feels about themselves, and that is actually what this book is intended to help you do. It will tell you the best way to keep away from a few of the most widely recognized 'nurturing traps', for example, over-adulating and persuading through remunerations, and give you compelling choices that will help you create and sustain your youngster's certainty and confidence and amplify their odds of developing to become glad and able grown-ups.

CHAPTER ONE

Normal Nurturing Botches That Influence Kids' Confidence

Each Parent needs to support their youngsters' confidence and certainty.

Notwithstanding, the most recent research shows that a portion of the things that guardians do with good motivations can be adverse to a kid's confidence, especially because our activities can make youngsters question our genuineness and cause them to get terrified of disappointment. Here are the 5 regular slip-ups that guardians make, typically because of a need for attention to their outcomes:

Utilizing evaluative recognition

One of the keys to building up a youngster's confidence is to cause them to feel better about themselves; numerous guardians imagine that the most ideal method of doing this is by guaranteeing that kids get heaps of acclaim and consolation. Furthermore, while it is genuine that a few types of applause and positive remarks made to our youngsters are prone to persuade them, research shows that specific sorts of commendation can cause more damage than anything else.

In reality, research proposes that utilizing evaluative acclaim with proclamations, for example, "You're not kidding" "You're acceptable at this" can make a dread of disappointment because youngsters become reluctant to do whatever could uncover their 'blemishes' and call into question their 'talent'. And yet such applause is usually utilized by guardians since it used to be prompted by nurturing specialists in the 'confidence-building culture' of the most recent decades.

Utilizing such evaluative expressions centers around our youngsters' 'inborn' gifts instead of their capacity to grow new abilities, and we risk confining them to embracing a specific character. Since, in such a case that a youngster recognizes as being 'brilliant or 'acceptable', they may feel like they need to satisfy that insight constantly, and this pressing factor can prompt kids to get rid of disappointment. Such pressing factor brings about youngsters getting less inclined to attempt new things or taking chances inspired by a paranoid fear of not getting it 'right' thus they wind up passing up fundamental freedoms to build up their certainty and self-appreciation. They are likewise likely to begin ignoring their folks' enthusiasm for them since they develop and become skeptical of this commendation and may question its genuineness. Maybe then causing youngsters to rest easy thinking about themselves, evaluative recognition frequently has the contrary impact, in that it can make them center around their shortcomings. Now, on the off chance that we tell our youngster that they are an astounding peruser, their response may be, "How might I be a brilliant peruser? It can likewise prompt sensations of quick forswearing and doubt: "I don't have the foggiest idea why they're lauding my drawing at the point when the one I improved - they should lie". Or on the other hand in a few cases, it can even be capable as control: "I haven't done anything to merit the applause they're giving me; they should just say it since they need something from me".

Even though we may utilize it with good motives, evaluative acclaim puts as well much tension on kids to satisfy our glorified view of their capacity and capabilities. To be sure, numerous guardians track down that the more applause they attempt to give as their youngster grows up; the faster their youngster is to dismiss them! This shouldn't imply that we ought to try not to adulate our youngsters; indeed a remarkable inverse is valid. The key is to applaud more powerfully in order to create a 'Development Mindset', as we will find in the accompanying sections.

Zeroing in on the result

On the off chance that we will in general zero in on the results by applauding them with articulations, for example, "I'm so pleased with you for getting 100% in your school test", we can incidentally disregard the exertion that our kids have placed in on the events when they try not to dominate or aren't effective in a test or action. As we will find in the following parts, the exertion that they put into something and the potential botches that they make when they don't get it 'right' are generally more significant encounters for creating confidence than the actual result. Likewise, if we possibly acclaim our youngsters on the off chance that they accomplish a decent result, it can cause them to feel like they need to take a stab at flawlessness without failure, and if they don't accomplish it then they are in some way or another weak. This strain to succeed each time can prompt youngsters to build up a drawn-out dread of disappointment. It can likewise make youngsters imagine that on the off chance that they don't arrive at the ideal result (scoring exceptionally in a test, dominating a football match, and so forth) at that point they will not get their parent's recognition. Furthermore, for some youngsters, this obvious retention of recognition can feel like an analysis.

Reprimanding and contrasting with others

There isn't anything more demotivating for a youngster than accepting a consistent 'diet' of remedial input or 'valuable criticism'. This can cause them to feel singled out and as though they're being disgraced for parts of their character or conduct. But then, it is very simple to wind up as guardians in 'blunder identification' or 'flaw discovering' mode, especially when we feel our youngster is being languid and isn't investing sufficient energy into an undertaking or action.

This is especially obvious when it comes to tests and grades. It is enticing to take a gander at a test and point out all the mix-ups and this is especially demotivating for youngsters. At the point when we center on featuring what the child has done well, all things considered, it helps their certainty and causes them to accept that they are proficient and that they will want to improve. At the point when you do have to give criticism, attempt to do it in a way that won't influence their certainty. See Chapter 3 for additional thoughts on how to do this. It is additionally fundamental that you try not to contrast them with a superior acted kin or school companion as this is likewise demotivating, and it could send your youngster the message that they have inborn blemishes and thusly have practically no limit to change.

Overpraising and going over the edge

Giving kids steady recognition for even the smallest of accomplishments may appear like a decent method of expanding their certainty, assisting them with getting more skilled and improving conduct. This kind of consistent 'positive support' is in reality a child according to various nurturing specialists these days.

Nonetheless, research shows that lauding youngsters unpredictably implies that our acclaim is probably going to be aimless to them and loses its ability to impact over time.

By being commended for all that they do, youngsters are probably going to become 'acclaim addicts' and be excessively impacted by other's opinions about them as they are so used to being evaluated. This additionally makes it almost certain that they will become 'accommodating people' as grown-ups who look for consistent approval from other individuals. Accordingly, they may end up now and again being either 'made' or 'broken' by another person's assessment of them. Essentially, if we become over-energized while applauding kids for the smallest of accomplishments, this can make them question our earnestness. All in all, if you go excessively 'over the top', you may track down that in the drawn-out your kid becomes negative of your recognition and begins to question the genuineness of the appreciation you have for them. Youngsters are truly adept at detecting when we are not being credible in our cooperation's with them, so on the off chance that we do this time after time, we may discover that it starts to contrarily affect the trust and association we have with them. This is particularly valid for more seasoned kids; while small kids will in general acknowledge what we say undoubtedly, teens are typically more mindful of the conceivable thought processes behind our words and activities. With development comes a specific degree of skepticism just as the capacity to address, so remember this while commending more seasoned youngsters.

Utilizing reward frameworks and sticker diagrams

Prizes and sticker diagram frameworks have gotten colossally well-known recently, guardians use them as a way to energize appropriate conduct from their youngsters and assist them with building up an uplifting demeanor towards day by day undertakings and family errands. While such frameworks can positively be successful for the time being, the prize outline framework instructs kids that the solitary point in being polite is that they will be remunerated for it. Undoubtedly, research shows that the outside inspiration given by the prize gets more grounded than the inward inspiration of basically acting the way they should. This implies that on the off chance that you continually reward your kid for something now; you are viably diminishing the opportunity for them to rehash that conduct again except if they are persuaded with more rewards. This can be hard for certain guardians to acknowledge, as remunerations and sticker outlines frequently will in general create speedy and noteworthy outcomes. Be that as it may, the change in conduct is probably not going to last because such award frameworks just spotlight on expanding the outside inspiration of the kid, as opposed to having any genuine impact on their convictions or disposition. This is because gifts or prizes don't urge kids to consider or assume liability for their conduct, it doesn't assist with educating them 'directly from wrong', and nor do they have any impact upon their good advancement. They are a method of 'paying off' our kids to do as we ask and once we eliminate the prize, the appropriate conduct vanishes with it. In the long haul, guardians are probably going to find that their youngsters generally expect more noteworthy prizes, so that when they become youngsters, they may decline to follow any of your solicitations without some type of remuneration like a monetary motivation.

Zeroing in on your emotions instead of your youngsters'

At the point when our kid accomplishes something, we're glad for, it's simply common to need to tell them thus, for instance, "I'm so pleased with you!" or "You've truly dazzled me" are two of the most widely recognized expressions that guardians end up saying. Although such expressions are harmless and good-natured, these are still assessments of our kid's activities and it puts the attention on our opinion about the circumstance without leaving space for the kid to make their self-evaluation. Youngsters could likewise decipher such explanations as implying that it's more essential to dazzle their folks and do right by us of them than it is to essentially participate in a movement for picking up, developing, and creating personally.

Effective Strategies to Manage and Control Anger

All individuals experience outrage. Outrage is an ordinary, regular feeling which helps us perceive that we, or individuals and things we care about, are being treated severely. It is an antagonism that we can feel towards individuals, however also towards creatures and idle objects. Anger can be an earnest inclination, which can emerge rapidly and demands us to act, or a gradual process that continually influences our contemplations. It is often actually just as sincerely awkward, as it has physical as well as metal components. Anger can be acceptable if it assists you with correcting wrongs, manage issues, and express negative sentiments. Notwithstanding, it can likewise be terrible, as it tends to be hurtful both to you and to other people, harming connections and influencing your capacity to succeed as you hope. The way we oversee outrage is a picked-up thing through life and is influenced by our encounters. Be that as it may, people are continually equipped for learning better procedures to manage outrage, to utilize outrage all the more emphatically and, to both recognize and stay away from, its conceivable unsafe effects. Be that as it may, on the off chance that you feel your outrage is or is in danger of, hurting you or others, at that point consider looking for help through outrage directing, which will assist you with comprehending the source of your displeasure and to put these, and other, procedures into practice.

What is anger?

Anger is a human feeling, with physical and mental segments. It advanced with humans as part of our fight or flight instrument. Outrage assists us with the understanding that we feel violated and gives us a desire to put things right.

Mental Health Outrage is ordinary and can be a valuable feeling. It isn't outraged itself, yet how it makes us feel and carry on, can make it into an issue for us and others. Anger is an awkward feeling. It includes expanded degrees of adrenaline (epinephrine), which make the heartbeat quicker, causes you to inhale quicker, makes you sweat, and causes you to tense up. Anger can cause you to feel all the more impressive, solid, and surprisingly unapproachable, and can quit you noticing torment. It can likewise cause you to feel defenseless, baffled, and small. The human reaction to outrage is to attempt to make it disappear, by using energy to 'use' the adrenaline. This can include showing hostility, yelling, or turning out to be violent. Anger can overpower other human reactions like sympathy for other people, so outrage can lead us to treat others, and ourselves, such that we later lament. It can make us act before we think.

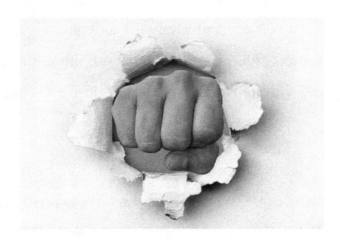

What causes anger?

Human feelings are not simply brought about by coursing levels of chemicals like adrenaline. Adrenaline levels are brought up out of frustration since outrage causes physical and mental (rather than sexual, albeit this can sometimes occur for certain individuals) excitement. Adrenaline is the dominant chemical of a wide range of excitement. Known as the fight or flight chemical, it is included in excitement just as dread, joy, and wants just as outrage and stress. Our actual bodies may react also with a crashing heart, perspiring, quick breathing, etc., yet our perception of whether we feel this as outrage (or as another feeling) is influenced by the thinking, processing, and feeling portions of our cerebrums, by our recollections, by our states of mind and by our personalities. Some of these cycles can be intentionally changed; some of them are profoundly ingrained, even programmed. They all favor how we experience significant degrees of adrenaline. Why do a few groups get more furious than others? Anger is something we feel at all ages, from little adolescence to incredible age. How we bargain with anger relies upon the amount it overpowers our typical reasoning and arranging, on how we have learned to react, and on what we decide to do. Some of the time we act before we choose. Anger is diverse for us all. The things that drive you crazy will be influenced by what matters to you, by your character, and by the encounters you have had. It is feasible to feel extremely angry and not show it by any stretch of the imagination. For the greater part of us, it is feasible to be overpowered by outrage; however, the circumstances that get this going are diverse for us all. What are 'issues with outrage'?

Individuals some of the time talking about having 'issues with outrage', implying that possibly you or others are uncomfortable with or stressed over your indignation, or that you are viewed as being irate more often than not is 'normal. Issues with outrage include: Feeling furious a great deal of the time. Feeling pushed, drained, and surprisingly truly unwell due to your anger. Having a 'short circuit' - responding with outrage rapidly or lopsidedly to things that distress or challenge you. Directing your resentment, the incorrect way - for example, at some unacceptable individual, or things rather than people. Displaying verbal or actual hostility, which may scare others. If you feel irate however can't communicate it, you are probably going to feel both genuinely and psychologically unwell. Indications like helpless rest, waking early, feeling disturbed, experiencing nausea acid reflux, and a crashing heart (palpitations) are common. Why will not my indignation go away? If somebody intentionally treats you outlandishly it isn't unexpected to feel furious. Frequently this sort of anger dissipates rapidly, and you quiet down. Sometimes, notwithstanding, the trigger for your resentment isn't something that simply occurred, but something broader in your life or conditions, or a previous encounter that is still causing you trouble. At the point when this is the situation, you may appear to turn out to be out of nowhere irate about very small things, yet the genuine reason for your resentment is something more profound, and 'moderate burning. This sort of enduring annoyance can be difficult to manage alone. It generally implies you have not been able to determine or grapple with the reason for your resentment. That may be on because you have been treated unfairly, and it might appear to be that there isn't anything that you can do to this. With this case it bodes well to find support. Advising and talking treatments can help you understand your annoyance and the reasons for your anger.

CHAPTER TWO

The ongoing research has made critical disclosures in the comprehension of what makes youngsters have the need to take on difficulties and why they can get scared of botches. Also, the impact this can have on their certainty, self-esteem, and level of strength. For a very long time, therapist Carol Dweck and her group at Columbia and Stanford inspected a gathering of younger grade students and zeroed in on how they reacted to laud. She found that youngsters incline toward one of two mentalities. The first is a 'fixed outlook', when a kid accepts that their insight is 'unchangeable' and will in this way just pick assignments that they consider proper to this degree of insight, in case they flirt with disappointment. The second and better outlook is the 'development attitude' having a place with the kid who is glad to take on new difficulties since they consider them to be openings for development and new experience, regardless of whether this includes committing errors.

Dweck found that a youngster's experience of applause had

an immediate impact on which of these mentalities kids were bound to receive. The main gathering of 'disappointment dreading' youngsters were, for the most part, used to being adulated for their insight with words, for example, 'you're savvy/sharp', though the subsequent gathering had all the more an 'attempt and attempt once more' mentality and was more acquainted with being applauded for their work instead of the result. As Carol Dweck clarifies, "Underscoring exertion gives a youngster a variable that they can handle. They come to consider themselves to be in charge of their prosperity. Stressing regular insight removes it from the kid's control, and it gives nothing but bad for the formula to reacting to a disappointment." The ramifications of a Fixed Mindset in youngsters, Individuals with a fixed mentality accept that their essential degree of knowledge, ability and capacity is 'fixed' from birth and consequently can't be created or improved after some time. So when a kid has a fixed mentality, this can influence everything from their demeanor to learning and schooling directly through to their eagerness to take on new difficulties or attempt new things. Youngsters are probably not going to partake in a movement, regardless of whether it is a game or something instructive, on the off chance that they don't accept that they can build up their capacity and improve at it after some time. They are undeniably more prone to stay with the things that they are acceptable at in the conviction that, that is the place where their 'characteristic' capacities lie. Since, supposing that they endeavor something new and don't get it 'right' the first time, at that point, this could fill in as evidence that they need knowledge. Evaluative applause is firmly connected to making youngsters have a fixed attitude this is because evaluative recognition 'grades' kids as indicated by their apparent level of capacity. For instance, on the off chance that we tell youngsters that they are shrewd, they may feel that they need to satisfy this impression of themselves constantly and will begin to keep away from anything that may raise doubt about their degree of knowledge, inspired by a paranoid fear of disillusioning us. Thus, they may begin to build up an abhorrence for tests and it can prompt them to hate, and in this way staying away from, training and learning in the long haul. As clarified, a mentality is a bunch of individual convictions and is a perspective that impacts our conduct and mentality toward ourselves as well as other people. Be that as it may, while it's critical to know about the contrasts between a development outlook also, a fixed outlook, it's similarly imperative to try not to classify youngsters as having it is possible. We need to recall that individuals once in a while fit perfectly into one class; we as a whole showcase specific attributes of every outlook contingent upon our disposition and the circumstance.

Slip-ups as promising circumstances for learning: "You are not a disappointment until you begin reprimanding others for your mix-ups" The other essential driver of kids building up a fixed outlook is a youngster's understanding of, and their mentality towards, the errors that they make. Making botches is part of being human, so if our kids fear making them, they will be less inclined to take on new difficulties and will be extremely impervious to doing whatever is new, which is not a decent groundwork for the real factors of grown- up life. It's imperative to perceive that our mentality as guardians has a critical impact concerning whether our youngsters can gain from their errors or become apprehensive of making them. It's just regular that as guardians, we need to ensure our kids from getting injured, feeling debilitate, or committing errors of any kind. We love them such that we can't tolerate seeing them endure, so we often end up plunging in and 'saving' them from testing circumstances.

While we may have good motivations when we intercede a lot in their exercises, we frequently ransack our offspring of the chance to get familiar with the priceless exercises that committing errors and the cycle of experimentation needs to instruct. "It's especially significant for small kids to get the opportunity to play and face challenges without feeling that their folks will reprimand or address them for accomplishing something wrong.

Additionally, on the off chance that we continually issue our kids with admonitions of the relative multitude of terrible things that may occur, we can make them restless about existence's risks. We unintentionally undermine them by showing them that we are not set up to confide in them and have no confidence in their capacity to adapt to/gain from committing errors. Expressions such as, "I advised you so", just serve to remove them further away from taking responsibility regarding their slip-up and additionally gaining from its characteristic results, also, makes youngsters less slanted to tune in to what we need to say.

Each youthful experience, when taken care of well, can turn into a significant learning experience. Permitting your youngsters to commit errors and experience their characteristic results instructs them that it's alright to misunderstand things from time to time, and therefore they will turn out to be better prepared, not just at taking care of their missteps but forestalling them in the long run.

By exhibiting through our actions just as we have said, that it is alright to make botches, we are assisting our youngsters with building up a development attitude. While on the off chance that we rebuff, chide or express dissatisfaction when our youngsters commit an error, they are undeniably bound to embrace a fixed attitude, which as we have as of now found, can contrarily affect their demeanor to learning and their capacity to grow new abilities. As a parent, it's imperative to have confidence in your youngsters that they can endure upset and disillusionment since they will turn out to be more sure and tough simultaneously. So for instance, when attempting to get them welcome to a birthday celebration they were excluded from, or forcing the soccer mentor to give them more game time - we're not helping them as we're eliminating significant freedoms for our children to build up their 'mistake' muscle. Children need to realize that it's alright to fall flat and that it's not unexpected to feel pitiful, on edge, or the other hand irate. They figure out how to prevail by conquering impediments, not by having us eliminate them. So what you should attempt to do all things being equal, no matter how hard it might be, is begin figuring out how to distinguish which botches you need to permit your kids to make. Such mix-ups are known as 'moderate' botches (instead of 'excessively expensive' botches that could bring about genuine surprise or injury), and by permitting your youngsters to bargain with the 'characteristic', for example, the prompt and legitimate outcomes of their slip-ups, implies that they become much better at recuperating from the mix-ups also, discovering approaches to tackle them in the long haul. To sum up, obviously our demeanor as guardians have a huge impact as to whether our youngsters gain from their mix-ups or get terrified of making them. So show your kids that it is imperative to accept botches by demonstrating this conduct when you make one. Furthermore, fight the temptation to plunge in furthermore, attempt to safeguard them from dissatisfaction and frustration, and rather permit them the chance to prepare and develop their 'mistake muscles'.

CHAPTER THREE

10 Ways to Foster Self-Esteem and Help Your Child Develop a Growth Mindset

Our research shows that instructing individuals to have a 'development outlook', which empowers an attention on exertion instead of on insight or ability, helps make them into successful people in school and throughout everyday life.

Building up a Growth Mindset in youngsters

What Dweck's and other neuroscientific research work shows is that the cerebrum resembles a muscle - it gets more grounded with use. At the point when we impart this equivalent message to our youngsters, the impact on their mentality and capacity to learn is astounding. Assisting kids with the understanding that the battles we experience when we are learning new and testing things are typical and are an indication of neural associations reinforcing in our cerebrums, is an amazing method to change their mentality and their viewpoint. Increment of inspiration, readiness to acknowledge new challenges, and better responses to disappointment are a couple of the advantages kids experience when they see how their minds work.

If a kid has been battling in a space of their schooling, by aiding them to build up a development mentality, we are enabling them to understand that on the off chance that they work hard at it, at that point they are probably going to improve. When youngsters get that their knowledge and ability levels aren't inborn but instead supported and created, they become normally inquisitive and are naturally spurred to issue address and procure new information and abilities through supported exertion what's more, difficult work.

Accordingly, our work as guardians ought to be to empower our youngsters' normal interest in their general surroundings and permit them to commit errors and learn through training, reiteration, and the cycle of experimentation. In doing this, we are expanding our kid's odds of building up a deep-rooted love of learning. Quite possibly the main advantages of a development outlook are that it makes youngsters more brilliant by showing them that their abilities and capacities can be created as there is nothing of the sort as 'fixed knowledge'.

Once youngsters comprehend that they can build up their insight by just taking a stab at it, similarly one would reinforce a muscle through rehearsed use, they understand that as far as possible to their capacities are the ones, they force on themselves. (The genuine illustration of Dominic O'Brien, eight times World Memory Champion in Chapter 4 is an extraordinary demonstration of this). This acknowledgment drives them to invest all the more difficult work and energy into their examinations furthermore, reinforces their adoration for instruction, implying that they are continually looking to find out more. So, we need to show our youngsters that the main part of any challenge is the exertion and practice they put in as this prompts them to have the option to accomplish anything. This permits youngsters to begin zeroing in on progress rather than agonizing over how well they performed.

Furthermore, when we quit overemphasizing our youngster's presentation and the result of that exhibition and spotlight on the exertion made, all things considered, we are additionally helping our youngsters to comprehend the natural estimation of just 'partaking'. This supports them to receive a disposition of 'exertion over result', which implies that the cycle of taking on new difficulties gets remunerating in itself, and along these lines, this becomes a definitive objective. Being Specific and making it about them as clarified in Chapter 1, we should be more cognizant and mindful of what occurs in the psyche of our youngster after we acclaim them. It is significant not to 'overcome' our youngsters with general explanations, for example, "This is incredible!" or "You're not kidding!" because when they detect that we are so miserably one-sided that we will respect pretty much all that they do, our acclaim becomes unimportant.

Our youngsters begin to question the earnestness of our recognition, and in the long haul our expressions of appreciation can blow up by making youngsters create a fixed attitude. Rather than adulating our kids with general/evaluative words, it is more powerful to recognize their work, conduct, or even their mentality. Commending explicit parts of their accomplishment in this manner will assist them with learning to self-evaluate their capacities later on. Thus, for instance, Dweck's examination shows that telling your youngster "You've done truly well, you more likely than not put a ton of exertion in this", is considerably more powerful than one more "You've progressed nicely, you're truly shrewd."

Frequently depicting something that your kid has accomplished, or communicating interest in the accomplishment by posing an inquiry about how they did it, is the most ideal approach to laud a kid. So for instance saying, "I truly like the way you blended the tones in your image", is better than, "That is an exquisite picture." At the point when we show our youngsters that their work is fascinating, it empowers them to 'self-assess in the future as opposed to getting reliant on our assessment or judgment. It is likewise significant to deal with our assumptions for what our kids can accomplish at various ages. In reality, over- assumption can without much of a stretch lead youngster to feel that whatever they do is never 'adequate'. Kids can undoubtedly create low confidence when censured consistently, regardless of whether the analysis seems, by all accounts, to be 'productive'. It is critical to refer to what they have progressed admirably and center on the exertion they have placed in (regardless of what the assignment), before discussing how they could improve and what they might have improved (see beneath).

7 different ways to cultivate confidence and assist your youngster with building up a Growth Mindset:

Assist them with finding their singularity:

Confidence comes from having a positive outlook on yourself and getting what you're acceptable at and at last what makes you exceptional. The best method of accomplishing dependable change in your kid's certainty and conduct is by expanding their inner inspiration. The initial step is to assist them with recognizing their special abilities. As they are youthful and need insight, it's essential to permit your kid to try different things with various exercises so they can discover things they appreciate and that they 'normally' have greater office/inclination at. This will assist them with taking charge out towards learning and improving, and they will be more averse to surrender despite trouble because they appreciate the action. As they develop, you can help them make a rundown of their abilities and 'presents' for the model, is acceptable at a game (football, acrobatic, moving, and so forth) or a melodic instrument, and this can likewise be extended to having attributes, for example, being an 'assistant', a 'carer', and so on. An incredible opportunity to discuss this is in a Family Meeting. The key is to guarantee that you feature their abilities in a manner that doesn't seem like evaluative commendation and doesn't zero in on their natural character. The thought is to cause youngsters to feel that they have the chance to build up the capacities and attributes that make them interesting. At the point when youngsters take part in conduct or movement only for the happiness regarding it, they do so because it is inherently fulfilling and not because they are attempting to acquire an outside remuneration.

Create tirelessness by discovering things that will challenge them:

Confidence likewise comes from battle and conquering affliction. It's significant that your youngsters don't just do things that come effectively to them and that they discover (age-fitting) challenges that they can survive or conquer. Empowering kids to track down their answers for issues essentially expands their certainty since it assists them with the understanding that they can beat difficulties without depending on another's intercession or commendation. The mindset helps them to persist through challenges.

It is hence fundamental to permit your youngster to battle when confronting difficulties as this offers them the chance to create constancy, diligence, and coarseness. On the off chance that they battle at something, as opposed to 'saving them' by mediating, you can help them by recommending choices systems to accomplish what they are attempting to do. On the off chance that they express dissatisfaction during a test and they say something along the lines of "I'm bad at this", consistently advise them that they are not yet acceptable at something. 'However' is an amazing word that is the embodiment of a development mentality versus a fixed one, as it reminds youngsters that this is an impermanent state and they can improve things with exertion.

Praise difficulties and missteps:

To build up a Growth Mindset and strength, youngsters need to feel that it's ordinary and imperative to experience difficulties and to commit errors as at last they can gain from them. One approach to do this is to help them comprehend that FAIL can be considered as a 'First Attempt In Learning' and that making a move and coming up short would yield less lament than neglecting to attempt in the first place. At the point when they experience difficulties, you should begin by giving your youngster compassion for their trouble or feeling (for example "You appear to have truly battled with your math schoolwork; math can be interesting once in a while"). At that point, you can help them discover methodologies to make things less testing, such as 'piecing' things, i.e partition greater difficulties into more modest parts to make it more feasible. On the off chance that you feel that there is an opportunity to get better at something they have done, rather than straightforwardly giving them 'valuable analysis', take a stab at asking them: "Are you content with the outcome" (as this permits your youngster to mention to you what they might want to improve on) or "What could you improve sometime later?". This will give them the freedom to self-assess and to be more engaged and liable for the arrangements that they choose to carry out to improve things.

Applaud the exertion, the constancy, and the advancement:

For instance, "I can see by your playing the piano the amount you have drilled", or "You know your occasions tables forwards and backward, I can see that you have put a great deal of exertion into becoming familiar with this". Or then again, on the other hand, you can request that they clarify the justification their prosperity - as it will normally be the exertion/practice that they've put into it.

Significantly, you acclaim your youngsters just for the qualities that they have the ability to change. At the point when you center around your youngsters' work, as opposed to their accomplishments or level of capacity, you urge them to get familiar with the craft of inspiration as you assist them with perceiving that occasionally errands expect us to put in exertion throughout an extensive period. You need them to think "Indeed, I worked truly difficult to get to this outcome so it merits putting forth the attempt later on". Urging them to embrace this demeanor will likewise make them less scared of committing errors as they begin to perceive that they are a fundamental piece in the learning process.

Acclaim distinctly and portray the 'interaction':

Zero in on procedure and the way towards adapting instead of just the result, and acclaim the means your kid takes as this shows them that each progression is an important part of accomplishing something. So for instance, rather than saying "Goodness, this is so wonderful!" ask your kid an inquiry, "How did you do this part?", or portray what you see, "Wow the chicken in your drawing looks so similar!".

Your kid will see the value in that you have looked into their work and how it was executed, and is bound to understand his/her accomplishments and need to share them with you.

Recognition explicit activities instead of their general conduct:

This permits your youngster to understand that their conduct is something that they pick as opposed to something they are. For instance, rather than saying, "You acted truly well when Granny was here", you can say, "I truly appreciated that you assisted Granny with getting and out of her seat during her visit." Additionally, 'organized' listening in - for instance commending your youngster to an accomplice or another grown-up inside their hearing can likewise be an incredible method to recognize one of your kid's particular activities.

Make it about them:

Finally, what you need is for your kids to build up their force of self-assessment and mindfulness. Without a solid degree of mindfulness, youngsters can become 'acclaim addicts' who are subject to you to advise them if they are progressing admirably. They can build up a sort of 'bogus self', which they embrace furthermore or adjust to satisfy the grown-ups around them or to get what they need from the world. To support your kid's capacity to self-assess and help them recognize their accomplishments, rather than saying "I'm so glad for you", attempt asking them, "You have tried sincerely and excelled on this test, are you glad for yourself?", or "Would you say you are content with the outcome?" What's more, when they answer, "Indeed I am", you can generally add: "I'm pleased with you as well!"

CHAPTER FOUR

Genuine Models: On How to Develop a Growth Mindset

The tales underneath are genuine models taken from a memoir 'You Can Have an Amazing Memory' and our involvement in one of our kids. These stories are incredible delineations of how kids and grown-ups the same can build up a Development Mindset at whatever stage in life and simultaneously, improve their certainty and confidence.

Genuine model 1 - How a mentality can change at whatever stage in life

This is the genuine story of Dominic O'Brien, eight-time World Memory Champion. It's an incredible illustration of someone who defeated analysis, individual difficulties with self-conviction, practiced and supported exertion and hard work and proceeded to accomplish perhaps the greatest accomplishments of mental nimbleness that the world has at any point seen. O'Brien had the mindset that if you center your psyche and put sufficient exertion in you can achieve anything, this had a significantly adverse consequence upon his confidence, and thus he became progressively focused and hesitant to go to class every day.

This wasn't helped by the way that his instructors were so baffled with his detachment also, evident absence of exertion that they would in a real sense now and again attempt to shake him out of his instructive trance.

O'Brien depicts how around then, he felt like his cerebrum resembled a muscle, however that it was in a lasting condition of unwinding and genuine peril of decay. His circumstance and emotions towards school didn't improve over the following years, truth be told if anything they deteriorated. The day he left school (at the most punctual freedom) he said it felt at that point, similar to perhaps the most joyful days of his life. Fast forward to 15 years after the fact and O'Brien proceeded to perform such a great accomplishment of mental spryness that it prompted him being delegated 'World Memory Champion', under eight separate events - he plunked down with a deck of cards and concluded that he would instruct himself to remember every single one. So what changed in those 15 years, between him sharing his educator's conviction that he would add up to nothing, to him choosing to plunk down furthermore, put his psychological deftness under serious scrutiny in a particularly outrageous manner?

O'Brien's 'memory venture' as he portrays everything started in 1987 when he was 30 years old and staring at the TV. The program highlighted Creighton Carvello, an achieved memory man of the time, recollecting a discretionary arrangement of 52 playing a game of cards. O'Brien was interested - he was so dazzled and inquisitive to know how Carvello had accomplished this amazing accomplishment that he plunked down with a deck of cards and concluded that the most ideal method of working out whether it was potential was by endeavoring it himself.

With training, devotion and hard work, he figured out how to remember that deck of playing a card game, and this prompted the acknowledgment that on the off chance that he set his psyche to something, he could accomplish anything. He acquired self-esteem and a degree of certainty that he'd never had, and he depicts feeling like a different universe of chance opened up before him.

O'Brien found that there are no restrictions to where a development mentality can take you, and his story exhibits how knowledge isn't something that we are brought into the world with and isn't 'unchangeable' as numerous individuals accept. It demonstrates that with exertion, tolerance, and difficult work, even the generally improbable of individuals can proceed to accomplish the most stunning of things. . This story is an astounding illustration of a Growth Attitude, and it is an extraordinary one to impart to your children to help outline the reality that knowledge isn't fixed and that you can accomplish nearly anything on the off chance that you center your psyche and put sufficient exertion in.

Genuine model 2 - Encouraging self-assessment and featuring the equal among exertion and expertise

At the point when our girl Noor was five years of age, we found all the astounding research portrayed in this book and we took in the significance of empowering our kids to self-assess. This implied that we not, at this point just centered on our own emotions about our youngsters, however rather we put forth a cognizant attempt to begin permitting our kids to communicate their sentiments towards us and what was happening to them. So we began changing our language and as opposed to saying "I'm so glad for you", we supplanted it with "You've been placing in to such an extent practice and exertion, you should be truly glad for yourself". Our girl's reaction to this was constantly: "Not actually, it was simple", whatever the movement. A half-year into attempting this, we were beginning to truly contemplate whether things are working with our little girl and we began questioning the impact this new dialect was having. In any case, not long after that, she returned home one day from artful dance and shouted "I'm so pleased with myself since I was named ballet performer of the week and it's everything since I've been rehearsing so hard!"

This was by and large what we had expected from the beginning - in addition to the fact that she felt glad for herself, which improved her confidence and certainty, yet she additionally comprehended that all the exertion and hard work she had placed in had empowered her to accomplish this. Half a month later, we took Noor to see 'Cirque du Soleil' interestingly, and she was hypnotized by the bazaar entertainers. Around ten minutes into the show, she came to us and said "Amazing, they more likely than not put in such a lot of training to be ready to do that!" We were satisfied to such an extent that she had arrived at this resolution by herself; she was showing that she entirely comprehended what it intended to have a development attitude and could see with her own eyes how much practice is required to dominate at something.

Furthermore, this significant learning is probably going to proceed to have a positive impact on her life for a long time to come. Concerning us, we couldn't have been any more glad for her, even though we did pick our words cautiously when illuminating Noor regarding this reality!

Genuine model 3 - How to transform misfortunes into a chance to build self- esteem and help build up a development mentality

Majority of youngsters go through stages of abhorrence or begin battling with one of their subjects at school or a movement. This is a typical issue and one that numerous guardians wind up agonizing over. The trouble is knowing whether we should attempt to mediate, and especially how we can improve things. We wound up in the present circumstance with our little girl, Noor, when she turned seven. Even though she had fused a 'Development Mindset' concerning sports like expressive dance, acrobatic, swimming and tennis and some scholastic subjects like math, it took us some effort to understand that she had built up a 'Fixed Attitude' concerning perusing and composing. She had been battling with her perusing the last school year, and gradually began to fall behind. We realized that she was battling, however didn't stress over it a lot as we perceived that all youngsters create at various rates, and we confided in the training framework to help her and energize her in the spaces wherein she was experiencing issues. We likewise perceived that there are nations where they defer perusing until a later age, so maybe she essentially wasn't 'prepared'. We additionally felt that if we dipped in and attempted to fix the issue, we'd blow the circumstance, mess up and most likely make Noor loathe perusing even more. The exact opposite thing we needed was for her to convey her abhorrence of adding something extra to adulthood.

We were stuck in a serious precarious circumstance, feeling uncertain with regards to what was the proper activity. The issue was that her hesitance to peruse was deteriorating. In addition to the fact that she was battling with the essentials, however, she likewise became truly on edge while doing it and in any event, when discussing it, particularly when plunking down to peruse with me (Nadim). Neither of us could truly comprehend what was making her so on edge and over the following (not many) months, regardless of our earnest attempts to support her, the issue gathered momentum until it kept her from getting into the school we had wanted. This was our 'reminder', as it was clear at this point that the issue wasn't going to correct itself and it wasn't only a stage that Noor was going through. Indeed, it was deteriorating so now was the ideal opportunity for us to act. We plunked down and discussed how we had managed the circumstance hitherto, and we before long understood that we hadn't permitted Noor to build up a 'Development Mindset' about perusing. Even though we'd urged her to rehearse her perusing and made time to peruse with her, Carole hadn't been steady enough for Noor to gain some consistent headway, which is fundamental in her inclination to be sure and growing more capability. We additionally contemplated what could be making Noor so restless when perusing with me, and understood that up to now, my restlessness for her to improve had made poor Noor reluctant to peruse with me on the off chance that she committed errors. All together for Noor to feel more great perusing with me, I initially needed to cause her to feel better about herself and commit her vibe that errors are alright. I needed to bring down my assumptions and put forth an attempt to be more tolerant and compassionate with her battle. We concluded that the most ideal approach to move toward the circumstance was to plunk down with Noor and include her during the time spent making a perusing program that we would execute over the late spring occasions.

Including her in this manner was an incredible method of urging her to open up and share a portion of the issues she had been encountering. Also, we realized that on the off chance that she had a say in making the plan, she'd be undeniably bound to adhere to it. By setting aside the effort to tune in to Noor and showing more compassion for her battle, we before long found that she was feeling baffled at the way that she wasn't ready to stay aware of messes with her age.

CHAPTER FIVE

Instruments and Activities to Do With Children to Develop Their Self-Esteem Top Tools to Create Confidence

Instrument 1: Limited Choices

Offering your kids Limited Choices empowers them to settle on choices from a youthful age and assists with building up their certainty. Albeit these decisions are for the most part restricted to two, this self-rule offers them the chance to communicate their personality and qualities, which thusly will assist with lessening power battles and struggle and make them more willing to agree with your demands. Restricted Choices works so viably, because it permits you to share control on your footing as opposed to allowing your kid to dominate. It shows them that you are set up to confide in them, assists with giving them a feeling of authority over the circumstance, and shows them that their assessment matters and that their emotions are being heard. Offering decisions additionally permit youngsters to work on deciding (between great and terrible) from the get-go, so it's the best groundwork for 'this present reality.

Instructions to give Limited Choices:

1.   Consider two restricted decisions or alternatives that suit you.

2.   Present these decisions before your kid gets an opportunity to go against what you might propose (for example before a force battle happens). This is the reason you should give Restricted Choices however much as could be expected for the day by attempting to supplant as many request/orders as you can with a Limited Choice (or other option devices like Asking Questions or Positive and Enforceable Statements).

3.   Request that your kid pick between your two choices. For instance:

a) "Might you want to brush your teeth now or quickly?"

b) "Would you rather get your work done now or after you've completed supper?"

c) "Do you lean toward the blue shirt or the red shirt?"

Instrument 2: Positive Redirection

As guardians, we don't generally acknowledge the amount of our association with our youngsters is as negative proclamations, for example, "No you can't have ice cream before supper", or "Quit hammering that entryway!". Truth be told, research shows that 80% of guardians' association with their youngsters is typically negative. Of course, we need to tell our kids 'No' every once in a while, however, the issue is that if we say it time and again, it begins to lose its adequacy over the long run and it can contrarily influence their confidence and trust in taking on difficulties.

Clinicians have discovered that by essentially decreasing your utilization of the word 'No' and other negative proclamations and supplanting them with more sure other options, you can have a huge effect on your youngster's conduct and inspiration.

Step by step instructions to utilize Positive Redirection:

A.   If your kid is requesting something that you're not able to give them:

1. Start your answer with a 'Yes' whether or not you mean to give the demand or not. This permits you to divert their solicitation. For instance:

• As a response to: "Would I be able to have a frozen yogurt?" attempt "Yes sure, you can have a frozen yogurt after supper" - rather than: "No, you can't have a frozen yogurt, supper is in thirty minutes".

• As a response to "I need this toy", use "Indeed, you can put this on your birthday list" - as opposed to: "It is highly unlikely I'm getting you this at this point!"

B. On the off chance that your youngster is accomplishing something that you need them to quit doing:

1. Utilize a positive order (likewise called a 'start order') communicated solidly and attempt to do this without raising your voice.

2. If conceivable, recommend an elective action or an

elective method of doing things. For instance:

- "If it's not too much trouble, talk discreetly" - rather than "Quit Yelling."

- "Tenderly pet the canine - rather than: "Quit harming the canine."

Instrument 3: Problem Solving

As guardians, we frequently jump directly to offering answers for our kids when they present us with an issue, or to executing outcomes or discipline at the point when they act mischievously, without allowing them the chance to settle their issues or to attempt to comprehend the purposes behind their conduct. In doing such, we are disparaging their capacity to take care of their issues, and we are not allowing them to take an interest in discovering answers for these issues for themselves. This instrument engages your kids to discover answers for their issues, instead of zeroing in on outcomes and discipline (which can effectively affect inspiration). It's an incredible method of showing your kid to have an independent mind and urges them to be answerable for their activities, which makes it undeniably more successful than some other type of control.

The most effective method to utilize Problem Solving:

This instrument can be utilized in two unique manners:

1.   Your youngster has an issue, which they outline for you: for example, they have no companions, they don't care for school or they are attempting to get their work done on time (which by the way is their concern, not yours):

a) Encourage your kid to take responsibility for the issue by asking them, "What could you do about this?" The response to this inquiry is as a rule, "I don't have the foggiest idea", especially on the off chance that they've not been 'instructed' to discover answers for their issues previously. So you can react to this by saying, "Do you need me to help give you a few plans to begin with?" or "Would you like me to listen for a minute to some different plans kids have attempted?"

b) If they say "Forget about it", say "OK, yet on the off chance that you adjust your perspective, I'm available to

68

listen."

c) If they say "Yes if it's not too much trouble, give them some various choices of conceivable arrangements. Offer them at any rate two arrangements.

d) Empower: After you clarify every arrangement, urge your youngster to assess it by asking, "How might that work for you?" On the off chance that you can't think of any thoughts straight away, just say to your youngster, "Let me consider everything and check how different children have managed this issue and I'll get back to you".

e) Show interest, yet abstain from meddling: Once your kid has settled on which arrangement they think would be the most fitting strategy (it is possible that one that you have proposed or one they have concocted themselves), all you need to say is, "Let me know how everything works out - best of luck!".

2.   At the point when you have an issue that you need to talk about with your kid: Perhaps you might want your kid to improve a specific part of their conduct and you need to

include your kid in discovering answers for this issue:

a) Initiate a critical thinking meeting: The best method of doing this is by accomplishing something that your kid appreciates or on the other hand, you can fuse this meeting into a family meeting. Recognize precisely what the issue is without accusing your youngster of the conduct while clarifying why this doesn't work for you.

b) Ask your youngster questions that show that you're in it together: "What could we do about this?"

c) Work along with your kid to create what potential arrangements there may be to the issue being referred to. Discussion about what you could both do another way next time the issue introduces itself.

d) Listen to their ideas cautiously, asking them: "And how would you imagine that would work for you?"

e) Have a meeting to generate new ideas: Decide on what you each believe are the awesome arrangements and afterward conceptualize together how you could execute them.

f) Ask your youngster how they would like to be reminded should they break your arrangement: If they don't have any thoughts of their own, help them concoct a fun approach to remind them.

Apparatus 4: Family gatherings

Holding normal family gatherings is critical to building and keeping a solid association with your kids and to building their certainty and self-esteem. It gives the ideal discussion were to give consolation and applause, what's more, to examine difficulties and how to beat them. It's likewise a method of ensuring that all relatives feel a feeling of having a place furthermore, duty towards each other, and it gives an important opportunity for every individual to have their considerations heard and their sentiments recognized. This in itself is unfathomably amazing as it assists with making an inclination of family solidarity and harmony and a more grounded feeling of trust in the strength of the family bond.

Instructions to hold Family Meetings:

1.   Timetable (preferably) one family meeting each

week.

2.   (Discretionary to make it fun) Elect two relatives to go about as Chair-Person and Secretary.

3.   Open the gathering with praises and appreciation. Every individual should take a turn tending to each relative to offer thanks or give praise. This is an extraordinary chance to utilize your new abilities to adulate the exertion and progress that your kids have made over the past week(s). It likewise altogether helps their certainty as they feel that they are seen and recognized.

4.   Request that each relative offer a second that they have been pleased with since the last gathering. Another extraordinary certainty supporter!

5.   Go through the 'Plan', which may incorporate at least one of the following:

- Individual issues, every relative has the chance to raise their need or then again recognize a difficulty they might be encountering.

- Hold a Problem Solving meeting to manage any

individual issues.

- Decide on an errand/errand framework: distribute assignments and family obligations.

- Plan exercises and family fun days.

- Play a game or have a sing-melody.

- It might sound somewhat messy, however, it adds to the feeling of attaching to end the meeting with a family embrace.

Different Activities that will help create certainty and confidence:

Creating mindfulness and objectives:

As clarified in Chapters 2 and 3, mindfulness is a critical part of self-esteem as it expands your kid's capacity to comprehend what they are acceptable at furthermore, to be reasonable about what they can accomplish. Defining objectives is likewise an extraordinary way to accomplish something throughout a significant period, as it assists with creating self-esteem and permits youngsters to commit errors that will show important exercises.

Here are a few thoughts that can help build up their mindfulness:

• Ask your kid (preferably in a Family Meeting) to share what they consider to be their most prominent strength and their most noteworthy accomplishment to date. Does their self-assessment match your assessment?

• Ask them to share a couple of objectives/dreams they'd prefer to accomplish in the following year. Get some information about the idea of this objective furthermore, how they will accomplish it. For instance, if they need to have the option to play the piano before a crowd of people in a year, or the event that they'd prefer to be part of the school's football crew, what are the means to accomplishing this. If they think of negative self-talk, discover approaches to show them why this is a 'fixed attitude' and how a development mentality can assist them with accomplishing their goal(s).

Showing them how their mind functions:

This can truly help cultivate a Growth Mindset as it shows youngsters that the cerebrum is a muscle that can be created. It's an incredible way of exhibiting to them that when we work on something new, the 'neural associations' that our neural connections make get more grounded and the simpler things get.

Improving memory:

As Dominic O'Brien's story illustrates, a decent memory can be an extraordinary certainty sponsor. You can assist your kids with building up their memory from an early age by playing memory games with them.

Here are two games that will help improve their memory:

• You have most likely previously known about the game: 'I went to the market and purchased'? This is an incredible method to create memory on the grounds that making a story around a circumstance is a demonstrated strategy to help individuals recollect things. One individual begins by saying: "I went to the market and purchased" and picks a thing. Every member proceeds and should recount what the others have said organized appropriately while likewise adding an additional thing to the rundown.

• Another pleasant and valuable game is to put 10 things on a table also, request that your youngster retain the items briefly. At that point inquire them to turn their back, permitting you to eliminate a thing. They at that point look at the excess articles and make some restricted memories (contingent upon their age) to figure which one you eliminated.

Showing them how to utilize their body to build their certainty:

Non-verbal communication can impact their certainty. In the event that you can show your youngsters to show certainty through their non-verbal communication, this will influence their perspective furthermore, they will feel surer, thus, at that point turns into a self-reinforcing cycle. Breathing is additionally an extraordinary method to build certainty by diminishing pressure and nervousness in instances of testing circumstances. Profound, careful breathing - which implies breathing from the midsection - is perhaps the best methods of lessening stress and permitting us to settle on quiet and objective choices. Relaxing for around three minutes out of every day since the beginning (and expanding this as they develop) is essential to rehearse with kids as it helps give them a feeling of power over their own feelings and responses to things.

How to Manage Your Emotions & Raise a Happy and Confident Child

Here's how.

1.   Set limits BEFORE you get angry.

2.   Calm yourself down BEFORE you take action.

3.   Take Five.

4.   Listen to your **anger**, rather than acting on it.

5.   Remember that "expressing" your **anger** to another person can reinforce or   escalate it.

6.   Wait before disciplining.

7.   Avoid physical force, no matter what.

8.   Avoid threats.

7 Ways to Help a Child Cope with Anger

1.   Teach Your **Child** About Feelings.

2.   Develop a Calm-Down Plan.

3.   Teach **Anger** Management Techniques.

4.   Avoid Giving In to Tantrums.

5.   Follow Through With Consequences.

6.   Avoid Violent Media.

7.   A Word formed or rephrased properly.

How does my anger affect my child?

It makes them stressed and this can **affect the** way **their** growing brains develop. Living in a household where there is a lot of **anger** puts **your child** at risk of mental illness later in life. Using hurtful words towards **your child** can make them feel like they are bad and worthless.

Is yelling at your child illegal?

While it may not be **illegal** to **yell** at **children** in a public place, it may not be the most effective way to parent and it may even lead to the discovery of physically abusive tendencies. Abuse is defined as physical, sexual or emotional mistreatment of an individual.

Here are some ways to show your kids how to be mentally strong.

1.   Role Model Mental Strength.

2.   Show Your Child How to Face Fears.

3.   Teach Specific Skills.

4.   Teach Emotion Regulation Skills.

5.   Let Your Child Make Mistakes.

6.   Encourage Healthy Self-Talk.

7.   Build Character.

8.   Allow Your Child to Feel Uncomfortable.

How can I be a more patient mother?

Taking 30-minutes to an hour daily to rest, exercise, read a book or whatever makes you feel refreshed will actually help you gain more patience as a mom. And don't forget to take mini-breaks during the day too if your patience is running thin.

What are the skills involved in parenting?

- Love and affection.

- Stress management.

- Relationship skills.

- Autonomy and independence.

- Education and learning.

- Life skills.

- Behavior management.

- Health.

What are the most important things for parents to do?

- Acknowledge the effort they put into everything.

- Allow them to solve problems on their own.

- Endorse and support curiosity

- Teach your child the foundation for success.

- Participate in your child's education.

- Give your child responsibilities.

- Help your child share his or her feelings.

- Provide challenges for your child.

What are some parenting skills and responsibilities?

- They teach more with actions (and examples) and less with words.

- They encourage more and criticize less.

- They spend quality time with their children.

- They act as responsible individuals themselves.

- They encourage dialogues with the kids.

- They stay connected as a couple.

- They understand their kids' love language.

How do you raise a responsible child?

• Start young.

• Show children how tasks should be done.

• Let kids show someone else how a task should be done.

• Be trustworthy and dependable.

• Apologize when you make a mistake.

• Give children a role or responsibility within the family.

• Expect them to make mistakes.

• Avoid nagging, yelling, and criticizing.

What are the roles of a parent?

In this **role**, you give direction, impose rules, use discipline, set limits, establish and follow through with consequences, hold your children accountable for their behaviour, and teach values. You provide the guidance that helps your children to change, grow, and mature.

How do parents affect their children's personality?

Authoritative parenting styles tend to result in children who are happy, capable, and successful. Permissive parenting often results in children who rank low in happiness and self-regulation. These children are more likely to experience problems with authority and tend to perform poorly in school.

How does parenting affect mental health?

Critical parenting has been consistently associated with depression and, to a lesser extent, anxiety. It is hypothesized that parents who criticize and minimize the child's feelings, undermine the child's emotion regulation and increase their sensitivity to emotional health problems such as anxiety and depression. I believe the relationship we have with our children is the most important element of parenting. It is the value of our connection that determines how well they listen to us, accept our limits and values, and cooperate. Good parents nurture independence, fostering personal responsibility and encouraging self-reliance. They avoid the trappings of micromanaging or indulging their kids, and they never allow slothfulness or laziness to take root in their kid's life. Children feel secure and loved when they have strong and positive family relationships. Positive family relationships help families resolve conflict, work as a team and enjoy each other's company. Positive family relationships are built on quality time, communication, teamwork and appreciation of each other.

CHAPTER SIX
POSITIVE PARENTING

Positive parenting is the process of helping the child and adolescent to grow and develop in an atmosphere of love and understanding. It is not permissive. It is based on acceptance and effective discipline. It aids the learning process of the child by the use of effective discipline. This manual was developed to help the parents to learn about behaviour and how behaviour can be changed in a positive, firm and loving manner. The definition of discipline and punishment will be reviewed. The way to give directions will be dealt with in detail (you can't give positive parenting or effective discipline unless you can give clear and understandable directions). There are certain guidelines for being an effective parent. These guidelines hold true for that parent that desires to be a positive parent. It takes time and effort to be a positive parent. It is too easy to fall back on the way each of us was disciplined. As a positive parent we must be willing to learn and to teach what we have learned to our children. As a positive parent and a good teacher, we would respect the child and learn to understand the child in relation to the child's age and emotional development. Positive parenting is a challenge. The result of being a positive parent is to have a child that has a greater capability of becoming an effective, independent, and capable adult.

The Difference Between Punishment and Discipline

Discipline is the sum of the parts. Punishment is only one part. Discipline is the process of teaching a child right from wrong. Discipline includes the rules, the guidelines, the love, the support, the questions, the answers, and the discussions. Punishment, in its positive form, is used to help children learn by the use of repeated expected behaviours.

Discipline (Or Punishment) Can Only Be Effective When:

1.   The child does not avoid the discipliner (punisher).

2.   The child does not have a hateful attitude towards the discipliner (punisher)

3.   There is a decreased need for future discipline requiring punishment.

4.   The discipline (punishment) is not aggressive and can be used repeatedly.

The Rules Of Discipline (Punishment) Are:

5.   It must be given immediately.

6.   If reinforces are taken away, then the child must be able to earn them back.

7.   Punishment should be preceded with a warning.

8.   Discipline (punishment) should not require anger.

9.   Reinforcement of the desired behavior should be carried out to completion.

Punishment Is Used:

1.   When the safety of the child is in jeopardy.

2.   When the use of reinforcement is not effective.

3.   When the problem behavior is repeated frequently and there is no appropriate   behavior to be reinforced.

Guidelines for Discipline

Discipline is defined as the process in which an individual is taught behaviour that corrects, moulds, perfects the ability to think, and creates moral character. –

How to Maintain Good Discipline?

1. Being consistent

2. Being immediate

3. Using no more than one warning

4. Following through

5. Modeling appropriate behaviors, saying "please" and "thank you."

6. Showing approval with contact (50 touches daily).

Ideal Discipline

1. Doesn't require anger

2. Doesn't promote physical exhaustion

3. Can be used repeatedly

4. Can be modeled

5. Has a solid research base

Basic Discipline Techniques

All discipline programs are and should be multi-dimensional. The ideas proposed in this workbook are meant to all be used together as seen fit. No one program, in isolation, will be enough for effective parenting.

Response Cost Program

While we're on the subject of effective discipline, let's take a look at precisely what discipline means. The term is actually derived from an old English word meaning instruction. Jerry Binger in his book on "Parent-Child Relations" suggests five essential reasons for discipline in families which correspond to the central themes of this workbook:

1.   Discipline teaches children to behave in ways that fit the appropriate expectations of the culture and insures them becoming effective individuals as adults.

2.   Discipline assists children in controlling their impulses thus allowing for the acquisition of social skills that enhance family and other interpersonal interactions.

3.   Effective discipline must be positive, reasonable, and temperate in nature.

4.   All discipline should be geared to the child's particular abilities and developmental level.

5.   As parents we must take time and effort to understand our children, their special needs, and the problems they encounter and need instruction for.

One of the most powerful devices known to parents over

the centuries has been known as a 'response cost program'. It means, simply, that if a child participates in a target behaviour that we want diminished, they lose something. This something they lose has to be something important to them, something that at least a part of them believes they can't live without. In other words, what children believe are and should be RIGHTS but what parents know are PRIVILEGES. A list of the things that are really privileges that a child might have within any particular family system could be:

1.   Playing whenever they want to (freedom)

2.   Watching television

3.   Playing some video arcade game

4.   Using the phone

5.   Having friends over to play with them

6.   Listening to music or stories on cassette players

7.   Going to bed at their normal bedtime

8.   Playing with a favorite toy

9.   Having Mom or Dad read a favorite story

10.   Participating with the rest of the family in a special activity

11.   Participating in team sports activity

12.   Getting a special treat before bed

Most parents know what their children like and so can modify what privileges a child might lose. The number of privileges lost and the length of time for which they are removed should be carefully evaluated. Most parents make the mistake of taking away too many privileges and for too long a time. This action turns what might have been a good learning experience into one of lingering hostility and resentment. For best results privileges need to be removed for not more than 24 to 36 hours and usually for less time in increments; e.g., one to two hours. The sooner a privilege is returned; the sooner it can be used again in the discipline program. This notion fits well for grounding, also. Grounding is best when used in small time periods, because:

1.   Grounding children also grounds parents

2.   Grounding for days or weeks is too cumbersome and parents typically don't have the resolve to follow through, thereby rendering the tool useless (especially for savvy children and most children are born savvy).

To increase the potential for success, charts are included in the Appendix as examples of how to remove privileges and actually keep track of the results. (Remember that if your child is upset with the discipline you're using, you're probably doing something right. And children hate these charts!) There are two different charts, one for children aged approximately 2 to 4 years and one for children aged 5 to 13 years. The principles are the same for each chart. At the bottom of the charts is an area to list the target behaviours that might result in the child losing something valuable. Next to this, is another to list the valuable things they will lose if the behaviours persist. The charts consist of seven boxes across the seven days of the week (eight boxes for the younger children).

Each day is a new day for the child with all privileges and all boxes available. If a child misbehaves, the parent has a choice. Take away a box by crossing it out immediately (or having the child do it), or give the child a first warning to make changes in the behaviour and then taking away a box if the behaviour persists. Usually the behaviour will persist, especially if the behaviour in question is a temper tantrum, so the first warning is primarily a parental weapon to allow the child to think there is some flexibility in the system and that their behaviour has power. In truth, flexibility is built in, but only to the extent the child performs adaptively.

Nothing happens if one box is lost. If, in the same day, more targeted behaviours occur, the same procedure happens again and the next box (6) is crossed out. When the 4th box is crossed out, the child is 'busted.' The buffer zone for misbehaviour has been exhausted and the child gets grounded inside and one additional privilege is taken. When this happens, remember that she/he is in close quarters with a parent(s) and that from a practical point of view the child should have some privilege left that would allow the family some space from each other; e.g., television privileges. Each succeeding box that is crossed out after #4, costs more privileges until there are no more numbers and no more privileges. The parents may opt not to take away a number and put the child in time out. Two discipline tools are often better than one. As children grow more accustomed to the program, they will view any loss as important especially for positive behaviour change. Behaving better is, from their point of view, now in their best interest. However, it should be no surprise if a child continues to lose down to the point where consequences get applied. This is typical for the child who has just figured out the program and decided to lose the buffer zone. But, without the buffer zone there is no room for misbehaviour. If the parents want to reduce the buffer zone, they can go from seven points to six, then six to five, but no more. In any response program, there should be the ability for the child to make at least one mistake a day; parents often make more than that. This program represents a reinforcement program, because the very next day the child gets all privileges back with a clean slate. The only time this might not happen is with extraordinary acting out the night before. If this happens, take up to all points away for the next day, ONLY. Remember, less is best and to keep as many privileges available as possible in order to have them to take away when misbehaviour occurs.

The Best Way to Give Directions

When you ask your child to do something, your directions need to be clear. If you are not clear, you cannot expect your child to do what you want. There are good and bad ways of giving directions.

1.   Use a firm voice.

2.   Before giving a direction, make sure you have eye contact with your child   and use a slightly louder voice.

3.   Model good manners when giving directions (for example: "Please take out the garbage.")

4.   State directions in positive statements (for example: "Please do this." not "Will you do this?")

5.   Break directions down into simple steps. Be specific.

6.   State the reason before giving the request.

7.   Have the child repeat back what they have been told to do.

8.   Place a time limit on directions. They need to know when to start and when it should be completed.

9.   Praise the child's actions when he or she first begins to follow a direction and again at the completion of a task.

10.   If you have stated rewards that will occur when the task is completed, then follow throughout with that reward.

11.   If you have stated a consequence that will occur when the task is not completed, then be prepared to enforce it.

Positive Guidelines for Living with Children

1.   "Catch them being good".

2.   Frequently monitor your children.

3.   Let them help you.

4.   Listen to your child. Every child has a special time to be heard.

5.   Discipline and enforcement of discipline should be as matter of fact as possible.

6.   Lectures belong in lecture halls, not in homes. Talking with your child is important.

7.   Show brief sympathy when you discipline, but don't give in.

8.   It is important to show your child or children that you can handle problem situations without losing your cool.

9.   Be a parent, not a martyr. Find a good babysitter -- not as an escape but as a breather.

10.   Parents are teachers: what you DO is much more important than what you say.

Keys to Encouraging A Child

Encouragement is:

1.   The confidence that I am loved for who I am and not just for what I can do.

2.   The knowledge that, no matter what happens, I am an indispensable part of my family. The assurance from someone I love that it's all right if I make a mistake because that's the way I learn.

3.   The conviction that I am more important than the problems I get involved in.

4.   The acceptance of an honest appraisal that leaves me challenged to grow rather than condemned to fail.

Encouragement focuses on the assets and strengths of our children, giving them the confidence that comes from feeling appreciated. Encouraging children helps them value themselves, believe in their abilities, and benefit from their mistakes.

Key 1: Accepting our children and ourselves as we are.

Key 2: Avoiding double standards

Key 3: Recognizing that Guilt doesn't motivate Key 4: Separating the Deed from the Doer

Key 5: Realizing that Comparisons promote Competition

Key 6: Recognizing unrealistic expectations and ambitions which Discourage Key 7: Making Affirmative statements

CHAPTER SEVEN
How to Raise Responsible Children

Teaching a child responsibility can help him grow into a sensible, dependable adult who's always accountable for himself and his actions. Learn how to do it by following these easy steps.

1.   Start young. Young children can help us set the dinner table or put their toys in the toy box.

2.   Show children how tasks should be done. Be clear with your expectations. Kids are imitators and they do much better when they are shown how to do something. Let's use those imitation skills to our advantage!

3.   Let kids show someone else how a task should be done. Nothing reinforces a skill like teaching it to another person.

4.   Be trustworthy and dependable. Children watch us like junior reporters, monitoring our every move. If they see us being responsible, trustworthy, and dependable on a

regular basis, they are more likely to conclude being responsible is just a given.

5.   Apologize when you make a mistake. Kids already know we make mistakes, so we might as well admit them when we do. If we own up to our mistakes without blaming someone or something else, we show our children there is no shame in being wrong or falling short, especially when we accept responsibility for it.

6.   Give children a role or responsibility within the family. It's important to give them a task that really matters and let them know exactly why it matters. If you have a dog, walking the dog is important for both the family and the dog— both sides are thankful!

7.   Expect them to make mistakes. It is so easy to forget, especially with older children and teens, that even though the body looks like an adult on the outside, the inside still has an incomplete operating system, i.e. their brains are not yet fully developed.

8.   Avoid nagging, yelling, and criticizing. As hard as it might be, we have much less conflict when we avoid

nagging, yelling, criticizing or other emotional displays when we are teaching or correcting.

9.   Work together as a family. Our children are not here to do the chores we don't want to do ourselves. Everyone in the family can take a turn doing the "yucky" chores, such as cleaning the dog's teeth at home.

10.   Provide friendly reminders to your children. Remind our children that everybody has to do things they don't like at one time or another; washing clothing is not your hobby – you do it because it needs to be done – and so should they.

Healthy Children's Needs

1.   Children need to be loved for who they are, not for what they do.

2.   Children need emotional stability rooted in hugs, smiles and kind words.

3.   Children need friends of their own age whose parents share similar values.

4.   Children need guidance in developing spiritual

beliefs and intellectual potential.

5.   Children need structured family activities with set mealtimes, reading at bedtime, participation in school activities and community events.

6.   Children need discipline of loving parents setting clear limits and who teach that choices have consequences.

7.   Children need time to have fun, to play games, to dream.

8.   Children need to be treated with respect and consideration including respecting privacy.

9.   Children need to be praised, to feel useful, to be given responsibility.

10.   Children need a chance to fail and try again.

11.   Children need freedom to share their feelings, ideas, goals, with parents who listen nonjudgmentally.

12.   Children need parents who openly discuss destructive behavior such as alcohol and other drug use.

13.   Children need parents who are reasonable and fair.

Children need parents who share their values and them trust them to make healthy choices.

Guidelines for Helping with Homework

Are you one of those parents who would do almost anything to help their child succeed in school? There is a way, but it's not easy.

The secret is monitoring your child's homework. How well a student does her homework is one of the truest indicators of school success I have found in my 29 years as a teacher and principal. The child who has homework regularly checked by parents and firmly sticks to a routine is more likely to have outstanding grades.

Here are proven ways for parents to encourage high student achievement. It's a long list and it is not necessary to do all these things to achieve good results. Adapt it to your family's situation and your student's learning style.

What parents can do

1.   In the earlier grades, go through the child's backpack as soon as the student comes home (or the parent comes home from work) to check for notices and homework. Check with older kids (upper elementary and middle school) to make sure it's OK with them. If it's not,

set up a system to make sure you see all school communications. Take advantage of fall, open house or teacher conferences to find out which nights you can expect homework. If the homework is forgotten, take the child back to school to get it or have him call a classmate for the assignment.

2.   Require your youngster to bring assignments home, even if the work was completed in class. If there's no formal assignment, use homework time to research an area of interest, read for learning or pleasure, or work at skill-reinforcement games.

3.   Set aside a regular time for homework, usually soon after the child arrives home, takes a reasonable time to unwind and eats a small, nutritious snack. If you agree on a later starting time, make sure it's well before bedtime and it allows time to work out unforeseen problems.

4.   Homework is done before television, not after. Some parents set up a deal so that for every minute spent doing homework, there's a comparable time watching television.

5.   There's a special place to do homework. This may be the dining room table or possible a desk in the child's room.

6.   Sit down with the child and review in detail what is to be accomplished in the day's assignment. Identify possible trouble spots and offer help if it's needed.

7.   Stay nearby, so you can answer questions as they come up. Some parents sit at the same table and work on home finances or other projects while the child does homework.

8.   After the homework is completed, check the work as often as possible, especially if your student is having difficulties. Never write on the child's paper and/or give the answers. (It's a long-standing source of teacher frustration that many parents actually do the homework.)

9.   After the homework is completed, checked, corrected and put into the backpack or book bag, let your student know you are pleased and proud.

10.   If It's a report that's due, help your student set up a time line to do the work over several days or weeks.

11.   Written assignments are more effective when done on a computer and printed on a laser or color inkjet printer. If you don't have the equipment at home, arrange computer time in advance at the local library or the school computer lab.

12.   Teach your child to be organized. Notebooks should have tabs with sections for each subject. There should be a daily homework record so the student and parent can see the day's task at a glance. If this is a weak area for your youngster, ask her teacher to help. You also could ask the school psychologist or principal about classes for improving organizational and study skills. Attitude's the key. What's described above is a family attitude about education. School is a very high priority. Little League, pottery classes, night meetings, social life, talent shows and just about everything else, while important and enjoyable, is secondary. If the family is called out of town, stop by the school to pick up homework for the days to be missed. It's not the homework itself that makes the child successful, but rather the importance placed on school by the family. It is best to start checking your children's homework when they are very young—as

soon as homework starts being assigned. This whole routine then will be second nature by the time the child gets to middle grades. Follow-through and consistency are essential at all levels. Another important aspect of homework (and of school in general) is to give kids plenty of chances to share what they have learned. Ask questions, and be interested in their replies. By the later elementary grades some homework may actually be too difficult for parents. Some communities set up a network of parents who feel confident giving help in certain subjects.

Conclusion

As we've seen, self-esteem and confidence are key to success and there are many ways in which we can help to develop these traits in our children. Being aware of the impact that our words and actions have upon our child's personal development and their sense of self is an essential part of this process. We also need to be aware of the most common parenting mistakes so we can avoid making them and prevent our children from adopting a fixed mindset. Because although there is no such thing as a 'perfect parent', there are steps that each one of us can take to become more effective in our approach to parenting and equip our children with all the tools they need to be able to thrive. Of course, there will still be difficulties and challenges along the way, but never despair. As the real-life examples in Chapter 4 demonstrate, there are countless examples of children who appear to dislike school and may be labelled as lazy and not 'capable' by their teachers and others, but who still go on to achieve great things in life. We must remember that as parents, one of the most important jobs we have is to show our children that we will always believe in them, no matter what. When we allow our children to make affordable mistakes and they see that we have faith in their ability to survive hurt, upset and disappointment, they start to develop more faith in themselves. And when we empower our children to believe in themselves, we also empower them to become happy and independent adults. So, when spending time with your children, keep the following points in mind:

• Show your children how to celebrate their mistakes by embracing yours as this will help make them more resilient and will increase their willingness to take on new challenges.

• Refrain from rescuing them from difficult experiences and unpleasant emotions - this will help train their 'disappointment muscles', and better prepares them for the realities of adult life.

• Help them to see that in every difficulty or challenge they face lies an opportunity for learning and growth.

• Always focus on the effort and progress your child

has made when participating in a task, exam or activity rather than the outcome as this will help them to develop a Growth Mindset and the art of self-motivation.

•   Be selective and honest in the praise that you give and remember to ask them questions to help them self-evaluate (such as "You must be proud of yourself given all the efforts you've put into this") before giving your own 'judgment' and praise. If you are consistent in the application of the tools in this book, you can maximize the chances that your children will one day - hopefully sooner rather than later - develop a growth mindset, find their passion(s) and become completely responsible for their own success.

CPSIA information can be obtained
at www.ICGtesting.com
Printed in the USA
BVHW091940140921
616745BV00003B/390